GUESTS OF ETERNITY
У ВЕЧНОСТИ В ГОСТЯХ

Larissa Miller

GUESTS OF ETERNITY
У ВЕЧНОСТИ В ГОСТЯХ

ও

Translated by
Richard McKane

Introduced by Sasha Dugdale

Arc
PUBLICATIONS
2008

Published by Arc Publications,
Nanholme Mill, Shaw Wood Road
Todmorden OL14 6DA, UK
www.arcpublications.co.uk

Design by Tony Ward
Printed by the MPG Books Group
in the UK

978 1904614 06 7 (pbk)
978 1904614 88 3 (hbk)

ACKNOWLEDGEMENTS
The poems in this volume are selected from
Between the Cloud and the Pit
(Moscow, 1999)

Cover photo: Tundra in West Siberia
by Pavel Altshuler

The publishers acknowledge financial assistance from
ACE Yorkshire

**Arc Publications: 'Visible Poets' series
Editor: Jean Boase-Beier**

In memoriam
Arseny Tarkovsky

CONTENTS

Series Editor's note / 11
Translator's preface / 13
Introduction / 17

Poems of the 60s & 70s

Poems of the 80s

Poems of the 90s

There is a prevailing view of translated poetry, especially in England, which maintains that it should read as though it had originally been written in English. The books in the 'Visible Poets' series aim to challenge that view. They assume that the reader of poetry is by definition someone who wants to experience the strange, the unusual, the new, the foreign, someone who delights in the stretching and distortion of language which makes any poetry, translated or not, alive and distinctive. The translators of the poets in this series aim not to hide but to reveal the original, to make it visible and, in so doing, to render visible the translator's task too. The reader is invited not only to experience the unique fusion of the creative talents of poet and translator embodied in the English poems in these collections, but also to speculate on the processes of their creation and so to gain a deeper understanding and enjoyment of both original and translated poems.

Jean Boase-Beier

I met Larissa Miller and her editor husband Boris Altshuler, who is a physicist and activist for children's rights, through two Quaker friends in the café in North London where I was in the process of writing my book of poetry *Coffeehouse Poems*. At that stage I didn't know of Larissa Miller's poetry. She gave me, I remember, some photocopies of magazine publications and, when she returned to Moscow, she sent me several books. As a working poetry translator from Turkish as well as Russian, I am given a lot of poetry in the hope that I might translate it, especially now travel to and from Russia is more usual.

What, then, made – and makes – Larissa Miller's poetry different? What was it that immediately struck me as a reader and gave me the strong feeling that I could, and should, translate her? It was not just that her writing career started like my own poetry and translating career in the '60s and extended to the present time – there are several living Russian poets for which this is true. It was not a *quid pro quo* act of 'friendship' translation although we did a reading together at the Pushkin Club when she returned to Britain some years later. There is a sensibility in Larissa Miller's poetry that is arresting and draws the reader into her poetry. She's a nature poet, a poet for all seasons, not only of the natural world, but of the soul. Her depictions of nature scenes, of snowscapes, are full of vibrant metaphors, often with images of darkness and light, evil and good:

> Oh world, your bodies are sinful.
> Your deeds are black at times.
> Be quiet and white, white and quiet
> at least between the lines, between the work. (p. 49)

And:

> When they led away the innocent under guard
> the cherry trees were blossoming tenderly,
> the waters of the lakes rippled
> in those black, black years. (p. 91)

13

Her poems are short, often with two fitting onto a single page. Some of her best poems address what it's like to be a poet, a wife and a mother – here she expresses her fears for her young son growing up in the Soviet Union:

Forgive me, forgive
that I brought you into this world.
What strength can
save you in the troubled hour?

These thoughts burn the soul,
my sleep is heavy, as though I'm drugged.
You dream though of daisies blooming.
Let them bloom for an age.   (p. 35)

And:

My child, the justification of my confusion...
I thank you warmly. You allowed me, the rebel,
to be your mother, tiresome and tender.   (p. 41)

Larissa Miller teaches English in Moscow – one of the most moving poems is to Yasha, one of her students who died.

His face will disappear in a moment.
And there are no miracles. But, Lord, until
the damp mound of earth has not yet grown
and snow and ice have not yet gripped it,
come and command: 'Let him rise. Let him walk.'   (p. 59)

Her husband, who edits all her books, also speaks English and they were both able to be of great help in the translation and editing of the poems in this volume, *Guests of Eternity,* which have been taken from her collection *Between the Cloud and the Pit.* This, like many of her books, is a selection of poems written over many years and its title, as well having a Dantean quality, suggests the proverbial "between heaven [sky] and earth" that describes the state of suspension that so many millions of Russians found themselves in for so long.

14

As to life itself,
you have no time to live,
you shouldn't even think of it
because there is a revolt in spring,
reforms in summer and re-elections in winter.   (p. 109)

Indeed, throughout the poems in this volume, we are aware of Miller's poignant, 'hands-on' attitude to suffering :

But whom will I ask? Everyone,
one could say, suffers the same.
What do I ask and about what,
if my neighbour is dying
from thirst by the stream?   (p. 37)

Although Larissa Miller also writes prose – essays and memoirs – it is for her poetry that she is best known; if I were to use one word to describe its quality, it would be integrity.

Guests of Eternity consists of poems written over a period of more than forty years and as such, it is an excellent introduction to the scale of Larissa Miller's work. For an understanding of the words, 'the Russian Soul', I can think of no better book to open than this.

Richard McKane

"However hard the world we live in, the hardest by far is to maintain order within that space, which is entrusted to us – our souls, and to see off the constant conflicts which arise on the invisible border between internal and external space."

Larissa Miller wrote these words in her essay *Man at Play* in 1996. They embody the spirit of much of Miller's writing. Whatever the circumstances, whatever the horrors of the external world, the state of one's own soul is of paramount concern. If one engages in the struggle to keep that in order, then everything else can be overcome.

This sense of uprightness, of pride and personal morality, pervades all her work and is felt particularly clearly in her memoirs *Dim and Distant Days* (trans. by Kathleen Cook and Natalie Roy, Glas, 2000). The memoirs describe with a lucid, and often merciless, honesty her childhood and adolescence in post-war Moscow. Post-war Soviet Russia was a tough place to grow up – thousands of Russian men had perished in the war and Larissa, like many other girls her age, grew up without a father. It was a time of terrible austerity: Larissa, her mother and her grandparents lived in a communal flat with other families, their local store served veterans and invalids and the long queue for food was made up of amputees. As a Jew, Larissa faced both 'casual' anti-semitism from school friends and officially-sanctioned anti-semitism throughout her education. Her description of these injustices, the child's own hot feelings of rage and bewilderment, are so precise that the reader quivers with furious indignation on her part.

> The teacher combed my hair, tied a big bow on my head and seated me in the middle of the veranda for all to see. On a clothes-line behind my back, my wet [bed] sheet was hung out to dry. I sat there with the pretty bow on my head until lunchtime and everybody came to have a sneer.

But in the memoirs the deprivations and injustices of the external world are contrasted with the love and brightness which

Larissa's mother, against all odds, manages to bring to their drab lives. Miller savours these moments: the little gifts from the market, cinema trips, evenings spent together. Her mother also creates the world of reassuring everyday routine: visits to shops, furriers, hairdressers, dressmakers and cobblers. Each of these exists in its own intact, magic world, a picture of cosy eccentricity. Despite the outwardly monolithic city, Moscow's 'village' community survives. From her mother and her absent father Larissa also witnesses that love may remain pure and may submit to no-one, and that it is possible to exist within the hideous Soviet social structures and yet preserve one's spirit unbent.

As Larissa grows older, the counterpoint between the outer world and a private spiritual world becomes both more marked and more terrible. Her mother and her few friends, poetry, dance and languages stand in contrast to a mainly vicious and yet apathetic society, to fear of pain and disgrace. And in the final pages of the memoirs, her much-loved dissident husband and their close circle of friends are tested by open persecution and imprisonment, before the final freedom and release of *glasnost'*.

I have dwelt on the memoirs not only because they offer context and detail to the poems here, but because the memoirs of a poet are always, however unconsciously, the outlining of the 'myth' of growing poetic sensibility in the poet. In her prose, Miller uses a collage of incident and anecdote to present the various stages of her maturing. Another essay, *All We Breathed In*, describes how Miller learnt to ride a bike as a child by cycling up and down outside Pasternak's *dacha*. Pasternak was also her absent father's favourite poet. His was the sole book he had taken with him to the Front, the last present he gave to a friend. Pasternak, she writes, is 'part of her', her poetic inheritance which she must grow into, and she expresses this visually: the child wobbling on the bike, gradually becoming more confident; the literary giant in his *dacha* between the trees.

Miller's memoirs, if read in the same way, show Miller's preoccupation with journey and spiritual growth. She is not born a poet or a person of spirit, she has to suffer and work at becoming 'herself' and she makes humbling mistakes on the way. In lieu of a conclusion she writes:

> Each of us, when we are born, falls into the river of time and swims with the stream, rejoicing at everything we find on the way, until one day we suddenly stop and ask ourselves: 'Who am I? Where am I going? Can I touch the bottom? Once you have asked this, you begin to flounder and sink. You stop swimming like a fish in the river of time and have to learn to swim again, which may take the rest of your life.'

This struggle to grow and mature with one's soul intact – 'learning to swim' – is what being alive is about, it is the only way to be. So, for example, Miller compares her own industrious, if not immediately skilled, efforts to learn to dance with the movement of a beautiful ethereal dancer, Ksyusha, who lives nearby. Eventually Larissa becomes 'a perfect sylph' and the unhappy Ksyusha is brought to the ground by severe depression.

Many of the poems follow this preoccupation with struggling and suffering. Take 'In this province of mourning and lamentation…' (p. 111). The question posed in this poem, 'Is it possible without suffering?', is answered with a finger at the temples (implying madness) in 'To rise to the heavens / pace after pace, night and day, / is the same as honestly / milling the wind' (p. 87).

The business of writing poetry is, of course, part of this suffering, a cross to bear, and one which must be borne with dignity. This view of poetry is perhaps alien to the British culture of poetry writing. In Russia, poetry has long been viewed as a terrible but distinguished burden, and Miller is no exception here. In 'It was on the very last day of creation' (p. 121), she speculates that rhyme was created by the Lord who began to sing upon beholding his handiwork, and his singing animated the soul, and the diverse words prayed for rhyme to unite them. So rhyme and poetry were created at 'the height of the Divine game.'

Part of the poet's spiritual burden is the duty not to stand apart from society and prophesy. This collection includes her political poems from the '70s and '80s which comment openly on the horrors of the Soviet system and the world. Particularly affecting in this respect is 'Everything happened that could' (p. 35). Written in 1974, it is a poem of maternal love and fear for the object of that love, 'My boy, flesh of my flesh, / my graft, having put down roots / alongside the black abyss…'. It ends with the wish that the fragrant flowers of his dreams should bloom for an eternity. Other poems comment directly on purges and tortures – none of them could have been published before *glasnost'*. When she wrote them, Miller would not have envisaged their open publication anywhere.

Miller's sense of moral purpose and her spirituality are religious in the widest sense. She believes in a God and another, and better, existence. Sometimes she addresses God in the poems, reproaching him, as Job did, for her difficulties. Sometimes this is an unorthodox vision, such as the little white-winged angel in the poem 'Don't scare off…' (p. 27), who inspires her to think that nothing that has happened is important, when there exists another realm of unlimited tenderness and all that is needed is to take a 'distinct and conscious step'. Sometimes the religious apparition is an unspecified and mysterious other, akin to a shiver down the spine, or a moment when one leaves the heated hut (see 'To go out once from fate', p. 69) for the 'black abyss of night, / and the secret reason of life'.

In such poems, poems of revelation, single moments when a transcendent world opens itself to the beleaguered speaker, Miller follows the tradition of nineteenth-century Russian writers such as Tiutchev, Fet and the later Symbolists – Bely and Blok. As with Tiutchev most of her revelations occur in the natural world – 'There is a surprising breach' (p. 71) describes a 'hole' between two nights which a stork flew through, carrying us 'bewitched'. In another poem ('The autumn wind chases', p. 57), 'A prophetic voice will be heard in the crunch of wood / and in the rustle of leaves'. Yet, like the Symbolists, she is not a poet of nature in the way we would understand this term. Her almost biblical landscapes are composed of trees, skies, wind and stars, rather than any particular observations of the natural world. Nor is she interested in local or rural dialect or phrasing. She uses consciously archaic and high-register words to stress the solemn and celebratory nature of the vision and in this, too, the effect of writers such as Blok can be felt.

In a revealing essay *If only there were no words...* (a line from a poem by Fet, which ends 'One could speak with the soul'), she begins by quoting Blok's poetry as an example of poetry which exists without words. By this she means that there is a poetry which is ruled by sound alone. The words themselves are simple, even banal, but it is the way in which these poems are linked with 'the flow of breath, with which they mix and to which they give voice' that makes them poetry. Miller's own poetry might well be described as 'poetry without words'. She uses, on the whole, basic words, unembellished simple concepts and objects – an analysis of her use of words would reveal the high frequency of words such as 'flight', 'tears', 'dreams', 'water', 'fire'. But her poems have an exceptionally strong lyrical and sonorous quality and a musicality which is hard to reproduce in English. She is an extraordinary technician. Her often complicated and dense rhymes and rhythms have an effortless quality to them, the 'unbroken movement' she observes in Blok's poems. All this creates the effect of a poetry which stands outside school and fashion and which appears to appeal to infinite worlds and gods. It strives to recreate in words the 'flight' and 'movement' of the soul which is so important to her. A few of the poems employ to great effect the traditional rhetorical paradox – calling into question the poet's ability to create flight, or to catch in poetry's net the essence of life, and yet doing so with such consummate skill that the poem appears weightless. It is hard to describe this to a non-Russian speaker. Russian is an inflected language, it has many rhyming possibilities and rhyme can be incorporated into a contemporary poem with an exquisite naturalness.

In Miller, and in Blok, too, the sonorous qualities of the poem, the songlike nature of the poetry is linked with the expressed religiosity. The intention of the poet is to create poems which enable the human speaker to lose herself in something far greater, the natural force of sound. In Miller's essay she compares this wordless poetry with the no less spiritual poetic world of Pasternak. Pasternak is a poet of words, she writes. In his poetry the words have a particular strength and energy. They lie 'across and not along the flow of breath', creating a new reality 'denser and more concentrated and expressive than life itself.' Pasternak's famous poem 'Vo vsem mne khochetsya doiti' (literally 'In everything I want to reach / the real essence.') is a good example of this – a poem in which the poet's longing to get to the heart of things, write exactly how life is, is expressed by a relentless attempt to make this longing precise, a repeated 'coming at life' with ever finer and more eloquent statements of poetic desire and frustration.

Miller ends her essay by stating that the poet 'has a complicated relationship with the word'. 'Sometimes', she continues, 'the poet stops believing in the word'. She writes that she herself loved Pasternak's poetry in her youth, but without ceasing to love his poetry, she moved away from him. Clearly her own preference is now for 'wordless' poetry, poetry which barely breaks the silence, barely emerges from it 'as the face of Christ barely emerged from Veronica's veil'. In some senses we can read this too as a journey – a religious journey through the poetry of words, through Pasternak and her younger self, to a poetry which, like a religious vision, barely surfaces from the veil of language. These new translations by Richard McKane more than amply demonstrate the linguistic and spiritual passion and commitment of this important Russian poet.

Sasha Dugdale

GUESTS OF ETERNITY
У ВЕЧНОСТИ В ГОСТЯХ

POEMS OF THE 60s & 70s

* * *

А у меня всего одна
Картина в рамке побелённой:
Июньский день и сад зелёный
В квадрате моего окна.
…И дуба тень, и дома тыл.
Забор. А ниже, где художник
Поставить подпись позабыл –
Омытый ливнем подорожник.

1967

* * *

Не спугни. Не спугни. Подходи осторожно,
Даже если собою владеть невозможно,
Когда маленький ангел на белых крылах –
Вот ещё один взмах, и ещё один взмах –
К нам слетает с небес и садится меж нами,
Прикоснувшись к земле неземными крылами.
Я слежу за случившимся, веки смежив.
Чем жила я доселе, и чем ты был жив,
И моя и твоя в мире сём принадлежность –
Всё неважно, когда есть безмерная нежность.
Мы не снегом – небесной осыпаны пылью.
Назови это сном. Назови это былью.
Я могу белых крыльев рукою коснуться.
Надо только привстать. Надо только проснуться.
Надо сделать лишь шаг различимый и внятный
В этой снежной ночи на земле необъятной.

1971

* * *

I have only one picture
in a white-painted frame:
a June day and a green garden
in the square of my window.
The shade of the oak and the back of a house.
A fence, and lower where the artist
forgot to put his signature:
plantains washed by the downpour.

1967

* * *

Don't scare off, don't scare off, go forward cautiously,
even if you can't control yourself,
when the little angel on white wings –
here's one more beat and one more beat –
flies down to us from the heavens and sits among us,
touching the earth with unearthly wings.
I follow what happened, my eyelids closed,
what I've lived through so far, and what makes you live,
and my and your belonging in this world.
It's all unimportant, when tenderness cannot be measured.
We are not scattered with snow, but with dust of the heavens.
Call this a dream. Call this reality.
I can touch the white wings with my hand.
I only need to rise. I only need to wake.
I just need to make a distinct and conscious step
in this snowfilled night on the unbounded earth.

1971

* * *

Ветер клонит дерева,
Пробивается трава,
Пробиваются слова
Точно из-под спуда.

Хоть и девственна трава,
Да затасканы слова
Про земное чудо.

Всё воспето до клочка,
До зелёного сучка,
Что колеблем птахой.

Что слова? Молчком живи,
Словом Бога не гневи,
Вешний воздух ртом лови
Да тихонько ахай.

1973

* * *

The wind bends the trees,
grass shows through,
words show through
as though from underground.

Though the grass is virgin,
the words about the earth's miracle
are worn out.

Everything is sung to the clumps,
to the green twig,
that is rocked by the little bird.

What are words? Live in silence,
don't anger God with a word,
catch the spring air in your mouth
and gasp quietly.

    1973

* * *

Так хрупок день – сосуд скудельный.
И, бредя далью запредельной,
Летят по небу облака.
Хоть ощутима твердь пока,
Но ей отпущен срок недельный.
И с талым льдом сойдёт на нет
Всё то, под чем таятся хляби,
И будет вешней водной ряби
Неуловим и зыбок цвет.
По шалым водам поплывут
Жилища, изгороди, щепки,
И облака невнятной лепки.
И распадётся наш уют.
И сгинут кровля и порог.
Взамен устойчивой опоры
Придут текучие просторы
Без верной меты, без дорог.

1974

* * *

The day is so fragile – a frail vessel.
The clouds fly across the sky
raving about the limitless distance.
Though the firmament is still felt
the time of the week is allowed it.
Everything under which the abyss is hidden
turns to nothing with the thawed ice
and the colour is uncatchable and shaky
in the spring water ripple.
In the crazy water there flow
houses, fences, chips of wood
and impenetrably sculpted clouds.
Our shelter will collapse.
Roof and threshold will disappear.
In exchange for staunch support
the flowing expanses will come
without true aim, without roads.

1974

* * *

В ясный полдень и в полночь, во тьме, наяву
От родных берегов в неизвестность плыву,
В неизвестность плыву от родного крыльца,
От родных голосов, от родного лица.
В неизвестность лечу, хоть лететь не хочу,
И плотней к твоему прижимаюсь плечу.

Но лечу. Но иду. Что ни взмах, что ни шаг –
То невиданный свет, то невиданный мрак,
То невиданный взлёт, то невиданный крах.
Мне бы медленных дней на родных берегах,
На привычных кругах. Но с утра до утра,
Заставляя идти, дуют в спину ветра.
Сколько раз ещё свет поменяется с тьмой,
Чтобы гнать меня прочь от себя от самой.
Умоляю, на спаде последнего дня
Перед шагом последним окликни меня.

1974

* * *

In the clear midday and at midnight in darkness and reality
I sail from my familiar shores to the unknown,
into the unknown I sail from my familiar porch,
from familiar voices, from a familiar face.
I fly into the unknown although I don't want to fly
and press myself more surely to your shoulder.

But I fly. But I go on. Every wingbeat, every step
is an unseen light or unseen darkness,
an unseen flight, an unseen crisis.
I wish for slow days on familiar shores
in usual circles. But from morning to morning,
winds blow on the back, forcing one to go on.
How many more times will light change to dark
in order to chase me away from myself.
I beseech you, at the dying of the last day,
call me before the last step.

1974

* * *

Было всё, что быть могло,
И во что нельзя поверить.
И какой же мерой мерить
Истину, добро и зло.

Кто бесстрашен – взаперти,
Кто на воле – страхом болен,
Хоть, казалось бы, и волен
Выбирать свои пути.

Свод бездонен голубой,
Но черны земли провалы,
Кратковременны привалы
Меж бездонностью любой.

Чёрных дыр не залатать.
Всяко было. Всё возможно.
Может, завтра в путь острожный
Пыль дорожную глотать.

Мой сынок, родная плоть,
Черенок, пустивший корни
Рядом с этой бездной чёрной,
Да хранит тебя Господь

От загула палачей,
От пинков и душегубки,
От кровавой мясорубки
Жути газовых печей.

Ты прости меня, прости,
Что тебя на свет явила.
И какая может сила
В смутный час тебя спасти.

* * *

Everything happened that could
and which it was impossible to believe.
How can you measure
truth, good and evil?

The fearless are locked up,
the free are sick with horror,
although it would seem they are free
to choose their path.

The vault of the sky is a bottomless blue,
but the collapses of earth are black,
halts are short term
among the bottomless chasm of time.

You can't patch black holes.
Everything was. All is possible.
Perhaps tomorrow on the path to the prison
you'll swallow the dust of the road.

My boy, flesh of my flesh,
my graft, having put down roots
alongside the black abyss,
may the Lord preserve you

from the drunken bouts of executioners,
from the kicks and the 'murder-bus',
from the bloody meat-mincer
of the horror of gas ovens.

Forgive me, forgive
that I brought you into this world.
What strength can
save you in the troubled hour?

Эти мысли душу жгут,
Точно одурь, сон мой тяжкий.
А в твоём – цветут ромашки.
Пусть же век они цветут.

1974

От жажды умираю над ручьём…
Франсуа Вийон

Научи меня простому –
Дома радоваться дому,
Средь полей любить простор,
И тропу, какой ведома
По низинам, в гору, с гор.

Но кого прошу? Ведь каждый,
Может статься, так же страждет.
Что ж прошу я и о чём,
Если ближний мой от жажды
Умирает над ручьём?

1975

These thoughts burn the soul,
my sleep is heavy, as though I'm drugged.
You dream though of daisies blooming.
Let them bloom for an age.

1974

* * *

I am dying of thirst by the stream...
François Villon

Teach me simplicity –
to be happy for my home at home,
to love space in the fields
and the path by which I am led
through the lowlands to the mountain and down.

But whom will I ask? Everyone,
one could say, suffers the same.
What do I ask and about what,
if my neighbour is dying
from thirst by the stream?

1975

* * *

О, разнотравье, разноцветье.
Лови их солнечною сетью
Иль дождевой – богат улов.
А я ловлю их в сети слов.
И потому неуловимы
Они и проплывают мимо.
И снова сеть моя пуста,
В ней ни травинки, ни листа.
А я хотела, чтоб и в стужу
Кружило все, что нынче кружит,
Чтобы навеки был со мной
Меня пленивший миг земной;
Чтобы июньский луч небесный,
Запутавшись в сети словесной,
Светил, горяч и негасим,
В глухую пору долгих зим;
Чтоб все, что нынче зримо, зряче,
Что нынче и поет и плачет,
А завтра порастет быльем,
Осталось жить в стихе моем.

1975

* * *

O mixed grasses, mixed flowers
catch them with the net of the sun
or rain – the catch is rich.
But I catch them in a net of words
and so they float past
and are uncatchable.
There's no blades of grass or leaves in it.
But I wanted that all should circle
in the cold that circle now,
that the moment of earth that captured me
should forever be with me,
that the June ray from the heavens,
tangled in the words' net
should shine, hot and inextinguishable,
in the dull times of long winters,
so that all that is seen now and sees,
that sings now and cries
and tomorrow will grow into a myth –
would be left to live in my poem.

1975

* * *

А там, где нет меня давно,
Цветут сады, грохочут грозы,
Летают зоркие стрекозы,
И светлых рек прозрачно дно;
И чья-то смуглая рука
Ласкает тоненькие плечи.
Там чей-то рай, там чьи-то встречи.
О, юность, как ты далека!
Вернуться в твой цветущий сад
Могу лишь гостем, чтоб в сторонке
Стоять и слушать щебет звонкий
И улыбаться невпопад.

1975

* * *

Неужто этим дням, широким и высоким,
Нужны моих стихов беспомощные строки –
Миражные труды невидимых подёнок?
Спасение моё – живая плоть, ребёнок.
Дитя моё – моих сумятиц оправданье.
Осмысленно ночей и дней чередованье;
Прозрачны суть и цель деяния и шага
С тех пор, как жизнь моя – труды тебе на благо.
Благодарю тебя. Дозволил мне, мятежной
Быть матерью твоей, докучливой и нежной.

1975

* * *

There where I haven't been for a long time
the gardens bloom, the thunderstorms crash,
the keen-eyed dragonflies fly
and the beds of bright rivers are transparent
and someone's tanned hand
caresses slender shoulders.
There is someone's paradise, there are some meetings.
Oh youth, how distant you are!
I can only return to your flowering garden
as a guest to stand at the side
and listen to the ringing birdsong
and smile out of place.

1975

* * *

Do these days, broad and lofty
need the helpless lines of my poems –
the mirage works of invisible mayflies?
My salvation is living flesh, my baby.
My child, the justification of my confusion.
The rotation of nights and days makes sense;
the essence and aim of action and step are transparent
from those times when my life became works for your good.
I thank you warmly. You allowed me, the rebel,
to be your mother, tiresome and tender.

1975

* * *

Казалось бы, все мечено,
Опознано, открыто,
Сто раз лучом просвечено,
Сто раз дождем промыто.
И все же капля вешняя,
И луч, и лист случайный,
Как племена нездешние,
Владеют речью тайной.
И друг, всем сердцем преданный,
Давнишний и привычный, –
Планеты неизведанной
Жилец иноязычный.

1975

* * *

Безымянные дни. Безымянные годы.
Безымянная твердь. Безымянные воды.
Бесконечно иду и холмом, и долиной
По единой земле, по земле неделимой,
Где ни дат, ни эпох, ни черты, ни границы,
Лишь дыханье на вдох и на выдох дробится.

1976

* * *

It seemed all was marked,
identified, open,
illumined one hundred times by a ray,
one hundred times washed with rain.
Still the spring drop,
the ray and a chance leaf
like alien tribes
possess a secret speech.
A friend devoted with all his heart,
a most old one and familiar
is an inhabitant with a foreign language
of an unknown planet.

1975

* * *

Anonymous days. Anonymous years.
Anonymous firmament. Anonymous waters.
I eternally walk by hill and dale
over the unique earth, over the inseparable earth,
where there are no dates, no epochs, no features or frontiers,
only breathing is fractured into breaths in and out.

1976

43

* * *

Пишу – ни строчки на листе.
Рисую пусто на холсте.
И плачу, не пролив слезы
Под небом цвета бирюзы.
Мой белый день – дыра, пробел.
Мой добрый гений оробел
И отступился от меня,
И жутко мне средь бела дня.
Пробел… А может, брешь, пролом,
Просвет, явивший окоём,
Счастливый лаз в глухой стене,
И добрый гений внемлет мне?

1976

* * *

Шито белыми нитками наше житьё.
Посмотри же на странное это шитьё.
Белой ниткой прошиты ночные часы.
Белый иней на контурах вместо росы.
Очевидно и явно стремление жить
Не рывками, а плавно, не дёргая нить.
Шито всё на живульку. И вечно живу,
Опасаясь, что жизнь разойдётся по шву.
Пусть в дальнейшем упадок, разор и распад.
Но сегодня тишайший густой снегопад.
Белоснежные нитки прошили простор
В драгоценной попытке отсрочить разор,
Всё земное зашить, залатать и спасти,
Неземное с земным воедино свести.

1976

* * *

I write and there's not a line on the page,
I paint and the canvas is empty.
I cry and tears don't come
under the turquoise-coloured sky.
My white day is a hole or blank.
My kind genius has gone timid
and walked away from me
and I feel horrible on this white day.
A blank... But perhaps it's a breach, a gap,
an opening, which showed the sky,
a lucky hole in a dull wall,
and does the kind genius heed me?

1976

* * *

Our life is sewn with white threads.
Look at this strange sewing.
The night hours are sewn with white thread.
The white hoarfrost is on the contours instead of dew.
It's obvious and clear that we strive to live
not in jerks but smoothly by not tugging the thread.
All is sewn with a very thin thread. And I live eternally,
wary of life unravelling the stitches.
Even if in the future there is decline, ruin, collapse,
today there is the quietest, thick snowfall.
The snow-white threads have sewn up the expanse
in a precious attempt to postpone ruin,
to sew up all the earthly, to patch and save,
to bring together the unearthly and the earthly.

1976

* * *

А вместо благодати – намек на благодать,
На все, чем вряд ли смертный способен обладать.
О, скольких за собою увлек еще до нас
Тот лик неразличимый, тот еле слышный глас,
Тот тихий, бестелесный мятежных душ ловец.
Куда, незримый пастырь, ведешь своих овец?
В какие горы, долы, в какую даль и высь?
Явись хоть на мгновенье, откликнись, отзовись.
Но голос твой невнятен. Влеки же нас, влеки.
Хоть знаю – и над бездной ты не подашь руки.
Хоть знаю – только этот почти неслышный глас –
Единственная радость, какая есть у нас.

1976

* * *

Погляди-ка, мой болезный,
Колыбель висит над бездной,
И качают все ветра
Люльку с ночи до утра.
И зачем, живя над краем,
Со своей судьбой играем,
И добротный строим дом
И рожаем в доме том.
И цветет над легкой зыбкой
Материнская улыбка.
Сполз с поверхности земной
Край пеленки кружевной.

1976

* * *

And instead of grace – a hint at grace,
at everything that the mortal is unlikely to be able to possess.
Oh, how many were drawn in before us
by that indistinguishable face, that scarcely-heard voice,
that quiet, incorporeal fisher of troubled souls.
Invisible shepherd, where are you leading your sheep?
To what mountains, vales, to what distances and heights?
Appear just for a moment, answer, reply.
But your voice cannot be heard. Lead us, lead.
Although I know you will not take my hand even over the abyss.
Although I know that only this almost inaudible voice
is the only joy that we have.

1976

* * *

Look, my darling,
the cradle is hanging over an abyss
and all the winds rock
the cradle from night to morning.
And why, living on the edge,
do we play with our fate
and construct a solid home
and give birth in that house.
And the smile of the mother
blossoms over the light cradle.
The edge of the lacy baby-blanket
has slipped off the earth's surface.

1976

* * *

Не мы, а воздух между нами,
Не ствол – просветы меж стволами,
И не слова – меж ними вдох
Содержат тайну и подвох.
Живут в пробелах и пустотах
Никем не сыгранные ноты.
И за пределами штриха
Жизнь непрерывна и тиха.
Ни линий взбалмошных, ни гула –
– Пробелы, пропуски, прогулы.
О мир, грешны твои тела.
Порой черны твои дела.
Хоть между строк, хоть между делом
Будь тихим-тихим, белым-белым.

1977

* * *

Not us, but the air between us,
not the trunk but the openings between the trunks
and not words but the breaths between
contain the secret and mischief.
Notes never played by anyone
live in the blanks and empty spaces.
Beyond the limits of the brushstroke
life is uninterrupted and quiet.
Blanks, omissions, absences –
not unbalanced lines, no roar.
Oh world, your bodies are sinful.
Your deeds are black at times.
Be quiet and white, white and quiet
at least between the lines, between the work.

1977

* * *

К юной деве Пан влеком
Страстью, что страшнее гнева.
Он бежал за ней, но дева
Обернулась тростником.

Сделал дудочку себе.
Точно лай его рыданье.
И за это обладанье
Благодарен будь судьбе.

Можешь ты в ладонях сжать
Тростниковой дудки тело.
Ты вздохнул – она запела.
Это ли не благодать?

Ты вздохнул – она поет,
Как холмами и долиной
Бродишь ты в тоске звериной
Дни и ночи напролет.

1977

* * *

Pan is led by passion, more frightening
than wrath, to a young maiden.
He ran after her, but the girl
turned into a reed.

He made a reed-pipe for himself,
his sobbing is like a dog's bark.
Be grateful to fate
for this possession.

You can squeeze in your palms
the body of the reed-pipe.
You breathed out and it sang out.
Is this not grace incarnate?

You breathed out – it sings
as you wander day and night
over the hills and the valley
in a beast-like longing.

1977

* * *

Иди сюда. Иди сюда.
Иди. До страшного суда
Мы будем вместе. И в аду,
В чаду, в дыму тебя найду.
Наш рай земной невыносим.
На волоске с тобой висим.
Глотаем воздух жарким ртом.
На этом свете и на том
Есть только ты. Есть только ты.
Схожу с ума от пустоты
Тех дней, когда ты далеко.
О, как идти к тебе легко.
Все нипочем – огонь, вода.
Я в двух шагах. Иди сюда.

1977

* * *

Все в воздухе висит.
Фундамент – небылица.
Крылами машет птица,
И дождик моросит.
Все в воздухе: окно,
И лестница, и крыша,
И говорят, и дышат.
И спят, когда темно,
И вновь встают с зарей.
И на заре, босая,
Кружу и зависаю
Меж небом и землей.

1977

* * *

Come here. Come here.
Come. We will be together
till the Last Judgement. I'll find you
in hell in the fire and smoke.
Our earthly paradise is unbearable.
We two are hanging by a hair's thread.
We gulp the air with our hot mouths.
There is only you in this world
and the next. Only you.
I will go out of my mind from the emptiness
of those days when you are far away.
Oh, how easy it is to go to you.
Nothing can stop me: fire, water.
I am two steps away. Come here.

1977

* * *

Everything is hanging in the air.
The foundations are a fable.
The bird flaps its wings
and the rain falls softly.
All is in the air: window,
stairs, roof
and they talk and breathe
and they sleep when it's dark
and get up with the dawn.
And barefoot at dawn
I am circling and hanging
between heaven and earth.

1977

Неясным замыслом томим
Или от скуки, но художник
Холста коснулся осторожно,
И вот уж линии, как дым,
Струятся, вьются и текут,
Переходя одна в другую.
Художник женщину нагую
От лишних линий, как от пут,
Освобождает – грудь, рука.
Еще последний штрих умелый,
И оживут душа и тело.
Пока не ожили, пока
Она еще нема, тиха
В небытии глухом и плоском,
Творец, оставь ее наброском,
Не делай дерзкого штриха,
Не обрекай ее на блажь
Земной судьбы и на страданье.
Зачем ей непомерной данью
Платить за твой внезапный раж?
Но поздно. Тщетная мольба.
Художник одержим до дрожи:
Она вся светится и, Боже,
Рукой отводит прядь со лба.

1978

* * *

Tormented by a concept that's unclear,
or from boredom, nonetheless the artist
carefully touched the canvas
and look, lines like smoke
stream, weave and flow
one crossing another.
The artist frees
the naked woman
from superfluous lines
as if from chains –
her breast, her arm.
One last knowing stroke
and body and soul come to life.
While they haven't come to life, while
she is still mute, quiet
in deep, flat non-existence,
creator, leave her as a sketch,
don't make that bold stroke,
don't bequeath her to the whim
of earthly fate and to suffering.
Why should she pay with an immeasurable
contribution for your sudden rage?
But it's late. The entreaty is in vain.
The artist is shuddering and possessed:
she is all radiant and, O God, she moves away
a tress from her forehead with her hand.

1978

* * *

Осенний ветер гонит лист и ствол качает.
Не полегчало коль еще, то полегчает.
Вот только птица пролетит и ствол качнется,
И полегчает, наконец, душа очнется.
Душа очнется, наконец, и боль отпустит.
И станет слышен вещий глас в древесном хрусте
И в шелестении листвы. Под этой сенью
Не на погибель все дано, а во спасенье.

1978

* * *

Куда бежать, как быть, о Боже, –
Бушует влажная листва.
И лишь непомнящих родства
Соседство с нею не тревожит:
Её разброд, метанье, дрожь,
И шелестенье, шелестенье:
"Ты помнишь? Помнишь? Сном и бденьем
Ты связан с прошлым. Не уйдёшь.
Ты помнишь?" Помню. Отпусти.
Не причитай. Не плачь над ухом.
Хочу туда, где тесно, глухо,
Темно, как в люльке, как в горсти,
Где не беснуются ветра,
Душа не бродит лунатично,
А мирно спит, как спят обычно
Под шорох ливня в пять утра.

1978

* * *

The autumn wind chases a leaf and rocks the trunk.
If you don't feel relieved you soon will.
Just a bird will fly past and the trunk will rock
and you'll feel it, the soul will awake.
The soul will awake, finally, and the pain will pass.
A prophetic voice will be heard in the crunch of wood
and in the rustle of leaves. Under this canopy
all is given over not to destruction but salvation.

1978

* * *

Where to run? How to be? O God –
the damp leaves in uproar.
With them the neighbourhood does not alarm
only those who don't remember kinship.
Their disorder, tossing around, shudder
and rustling, rustling:
'Do you remember? Do you? You are connected with
the past through dreams and waking. You'll not get away.
Do you remember?' I remember. Let me go.
Don't lament. Don't cry over my ear.
I want to go to where it's dense, remote,
dark, as in the cradle, as in the cupped hands
where the winds don't blow crazily,
the soul doesn't walk in its sleep,
but sleeps peacefully as people usually sleep
under the rustle of the downpour at five in the morning.

1978

На смерть Яши К.

Встань, Яшка, встань. Не умирай. Как можно!
Бесчеловечно это и безбожно,
Безжалостно ребенком умирать.
Открой глаза и погляди на мать.
Ты погляди, что с матерью наделал.
Она твое бесчувственное тело
Все гладит и не сводит глаз с лица.
И волосы седые у отца.
Он поправляет на тебе рубашку
И повторяет: "Яшка, сын мой, Яшка".
И повторяет: "Яшка, мой сынок".
Гора цветов. Венок. Еще венок.
…Пришел ко мне смешливым второклашкой.
Нос вытирал дырявой промокашкой.
И мы с тобой учили "I and You",
"I cry, I sing" – я плачу, я пою.
Как жить теперь на свете. Жить попробуй,
Когда вот-вот опустят крышку гроба,
В котором мальчик, давний ученик.
Его лицо исчезнет через миг.
И нет чудес. Но, Господи, покуда
Еще не наросла сырая груда
Земли, не придавили снег и лед,
Приди, вели: "Пусть встанет. Пусть идет".

1979

* * *

Get up Yashka, rise up. Don't die. How could you!
It's inhuman, godless.
It's cruel to die as a child.
Open your eyes and look at your mother.
Look what you've done to your mother.
She keeps stroking your feelingless body
and doesn't take her eyes off your face.
You father's hair has gone grey.
He fusses with the shirt you have on
and repeats: 'Yashka, my son, Yashka.'
And over and over: 'Yashka, my little boy.'
A mountain of flowers. One wreath and another.
You came to me as a fun-loving schoolchild.
You wiped your nose on blotting-paper with holes in it.
I taught you the English for 'I and You'
'I cry, I sing'.
How to live now in this world? Try to live,
when right now they are lowering the lid of the coffin
in which is a boy, an old pupil.
His face will disappear in a moment.
And there are no miracles. But, Lord, until
the damp mound of earth has not yet grown
and snow and ice have not yet gripped it,
come and command: 'Let him rise. Let him walk.'

1979

* * *

Опять это темп – злополучное "presto"
И шалые души срываются с места,
И мчатся, сшибаясь, во мгле и в пыли,
Как будто бы что-то завидев вдали,
Как будто вдали разрешенье, развязка,
И вмиг прекратится безумная пляска.
Неужто весь этот порыв и угар
Всего лишь музыка – бемоль и бекар;
Неужто наступит покой, передышка
И ляжет на клавиши черная крышка?…
Неужто два такта всего до конца?
Семь нот в звукоряде. Семь дней у творца.
И нечто такое творится с басами,
Что воды гудят и земля с небесами.

1979

* * *

That tempo again – a malevolent *presto*
and crazy souls tear themselves from the place
and rush, colliding in the murk and dust
as though they had seen something in the distance,
as though there was in the distance a permission, a *dénouement*
and in a moment the mad dance ceases.
Is all this upsurge and thrust
really only music – flats and naturals;
will peace really come, a breather,
and the black lid will close on the keys?
Are there really only two beats to the end?
Seven notes in a scale. Seven days of the Creator.
And something incredible is created by the basses
so that the waters boom and earth does too with the heavens.

1979

POEMS OF THE 80s

* * *

Между облаком и ямой,
Меж берёзой и осиной,
Между жизнью лучшей самой
И совсем невыносимой,
Под высоким небосводом
Непрестанные качели
Между Босховским уродом
И весною Боттичелли.

1980

* * *

Ритенуто, ритенуто,
Дли блаженные минуты,
Не сбивайся, не спеши,
Слушай шорохи в тиши.
Дольче, дольче, нежно, нежно…
Ты увидишь, жизнь безбрежна
И такая сладость в ней…
Но плавней, плавней, плавней.

1980

* * *

Between the cloud and the pit,
betwixt the birch and the aspen,
between the best of life
and the completely unbearable
under the high vault of the sky
the unstoppable swings
between Bosch's freaks
and Botticelli's spring.

1980

* * *

Ritenuto, ritenuto
let the blissful minutes go on,
don't interrupt, don't hurry,
listen to the whispers in the silence.
Dolce, dolce, tender, tender…
You'll see, life is boundless
with such sweetness in it…
But more graceful, smoother, more rhythmical.

1980

* * *

Благие вести у меня.
Есть у меня благие вести:
Ещё мы целы и на месте
К концу сбесившегося дня;

На тверди, где судьба лиха
И не щадит ни уз, ни крова,
Ещё искать способны слово,
Всего лишь слово для стиха.

1980

* * *

Неслыханный случай. Неслыханный случай:
Листва надо мной золотистою тучей.
Неслыханный случай. Чудес чудеса:
Сквозь желтые листья видны небеса.
Удача и праздник, и случай счастливый:
Струится река под плакучею ивой.
Неслыханный случай. Один на века:
Под ивой плакучей струится река.

1980

* * *

I have good news.
This is the good news,
we've still survived and are in place,
at the end of this berserk day;

on the solid earth where evil fate
has no mercy for ties or homes,
we're still capable of searching for the word,
for just a word for a poem.

1980

* * *

An unprecedented event. An unheard-of occurrence:
the leaves over me are a golden cloud.
An unprecedented event. Wonders of wonders:
the heavens can be glimpsed through the yellow leaves.
A holiday, a success and a happy event:
the river streams under the weeping willow.
An unprecedented event. Once a century:
the river streams under the weeping willow.

1980

* * *

Любовь до гроба.
Жизнь до гроба.
Что дальше – сообщат особо.
И если есть там что-нибудь,
Узнаешь. А пока – забудь.
Забудь и помни только это:
Поля с рассвета до рассвета,
Глаза поднимешь – небеса,
Опустишь – травы и роса.

1980

* * *

Однажды выйти из судьбы,
Как из натопленой избы
В холодные выходят сени,
Где вещи, зыбкие, как тени,
Стоят, где глуше голоса,
Слышнее ветры и леса,
И ночи черная пучина,
И жизни тайная причина.

1980

* * *

Love to the grave.
Life to the grave.
They'll inform you specially of what there is beyond.
And if there is anything there,
you'll find out. Meanwhile just forget.
Forget and remember just this:
the fields from dawn to dawn,
you lift your eyes and there are the heavens,
you lower them and the grass and dew are there.

1980

* * *

To go out once from fate
as from a heated hut
people go out into the cold porch
where things, shaky as shadows,
stand, where a voice is more muffled,
where the wind and forest are more audible,
where there is the black abyss of night,
and the secret reason of life.

1980

* * *

Есть удивительная брешь
В небытии, лазейка меж
Двумя ночами, тьмой и тьмой,
Пробоина, где снег зимой,
И дождик осенью; пролом,
Куда влетел, шурша крылом,
Огромный аист как-то раз,
Неся завороженных нас.

1981

* * *

Ещё пролёт, ещё ступени,
Войду – и рухну на колени!
Ещё пролёт – и дверь рывком
Открою. Господи, о ком,
О ком тоскую, с кем в разлуке
Живу, кому слезами руки
Залью. Кому почти без сил
Шепчу: "Зачем ты отпустил,
Зачем пустил меня скитаться,
Вперёд спешить, назад кидаться,
Зачем", – шепчу. И в горле ком.
…Ещё ступенька, и рывком
Открою двери. И ни звука…
Такая долгая разлука.
Открою дверь – и свет рекой.
Войду и рухну. И покой.

1981

* * *

There is a surprising breach
in non-existence, a loophole between
two nights, darkness and darkness,
a hole, where there's snow in winter
and light rain in autumn; a gap
through which a huge stork once flew,
with its wings rustling,
carrying us bewitched.

1981

* * *

Another flight, more steps,
I go in and collapse on my knees!
Another flight and I open the door
with a jerk. O Lord, for whom am I,
for whom am I longing, with whom am I living
in parting, whose hands will I flood
with tears? To whom do I whisper
so weakly: 'Why did you release me,
why did you let me go onto the road,
to hurry ahead, to rush back,
why?' I whisper with a lump in my throat.
Another step, and I will open the door
with a jerk. No sound…
Such a long parting.
I will open the door and the light is like a river.
I will go in and collapse. Then peace.

1981

* * *

Говорим, говорим –
Только дыма колечки.
Невесомы, как дым,
Словеса и словечки.

Крепко держим стило –
Пишем фразу за фразой.
Написали – бело,
Словно tabula rasa.

Краской той, что густа,
Размалёвана густо
Вся поверхность холста
Отодвинулись – пусто.

Что за сладостный труд,
С каждым днём осторожней
Наполняем сосуд
Безнадёжно порожний.

1981

* * *

We talk and talk –
only smoke rings.
Words, little words
are weightless as smoke.

We will hold fast the pen –
we write phrase after phrase.
We've written and it's white,
like a *tabula rasa*.

All the surface of the canvas,
thickly daubed
with thick paint
moved away – it's empty.

What a sweet job:
more cautiously with every day
we fill the vessel
that is hopelessly empty.

   1981

* * *

Чьи-то руки взметнулись над стылой водой.
Как бы дело не кончилось страшной бедой,
Как бы кто-то в отчаяньи или в бреду
Не пропал в зачарованном этом пруду.
Сбереги его душу, Господь, сбереги…
По осенней воде разбежались круги…
Чьи же руки вздымались? И голос был чей?
И кому целый лес запылавших свечей?

1981

* * *

Мы у вечности в гостях
Ставим избу на костях.
Ставим избу на погосте
И зовем друг друга в гости:
"Приходи же, милый гость,
Вешай кепочку на гвоздь".
И висит в прихожей кепка.
И стоит избушка крепко.
В доме радость и уют.
В доме пляшут и поют,
Топят печь сухим поленом.
И почти не пахнет тленом.

1981

* * *

Someone's hands flap over the icy water.
I fear the matter may finish with a terrible disaster,
I fear that someone in desperation or madness
may disappear in this bewitched pond.
Preserve his soul, Lord, preserve it...
Circles widen in the autumn water...
Whose hands rose? Whose voice was it?
For whom is this whole forest of flaming candles?

1981

* * *

We are guests of eternity
and we build the hut on bones,
we build the hut on a graveyard
and invite each other to visit:
'Come, dear guest,
hang your cap on the nail'.
The cap is hung in the hall.
The hut stands firm.
There is joy and shelter in the house.
They sing and dance in the house.
They stoke the stove with dry logs
and there is almost no smell of decay.

1981

* * *

Ты сброшен в пропасть – ты рождён.
Ты ни к чему не пригвождён.
Ты сброшен в пропасть, так лети.
Лети, цепляясь по пути
За край небесной синевы,
За горсть желтеющей травы,
За луч, что меркнет помелькав,
За чей-то локоть и рукав.

1981

* * *

– Ты куда? Не пойму, хоть убей.
Голос твой все слабей и слабей.
Ты куда?
     – На Кудыкину гору
Белоснежных гонять голубей.
Ты живи на земле, не робей.
На земле хорошо в эту пору.
Нынче осень. А скоро зима.
Той зимою, ты помнишь сама,
Снег валил на деревья и крышу.
На деревья, дорогу, дома…
Мы с тобою сходили с ума,
Помнишь?
     – Да, но едва тебя слышу.

1982

* * *

You are thrown into the abyss – you are born.
You are not nailed to anything.
You are thrown into the abyss, so fly.
Fly, catching on your way
the edge of the heavens' blue,
the handful of yellowing grass,
the ray that darkens when it has flashed,
then someone's elbow and sleeve.

1981

* * *

'Where are you going? Blow me if I can understand.
Your voice is weaker and weaker.
Where are you going?'
                    'To the back of beyond,
to chase the snow-white doves.
Live on earth, don't be timid.
It's good to be on earth at such a time.
It's autumn now. Soon winter.
In that winter you will remember
the snow piled on trees and roofs,
on trees, the road, houses...
You and I went crazy,
do you remember?'
                    'Yes but I can hardly hear you.'

1982

* * *

И не осмыслить в словесах,
И не измерить здешней меркой –
В бездонность маленькою дверкой
Сияет просинь в небесах.

Сияет просинь в небесах,
Зияет пропуск буквы в слове.
Не надо с ручкой наготове
Стоять у буквы на часах.

Пространство, пропуск, забытьё…
Лишь тот земную жизнь осилит,
Кто будет поражен навылет
Непостижимостью ее.

В пустом пространстве ветер дик…
Попробуй жить в стабильность веря:
Что ни мгновение – потеря.
Что ни мгновение – тайник.

1982

* * *

Not to make sense in words,
not to measure by any measurement from here –
a bluish tinge shines in the heavens
like a small gate into the depths.

The bluish tinge shines in the heavens,
the missing letter in the word yawns.
No need to guard the letter
with a ready pen.

Space, blank, drowsiness…
Only that person will overpower life on earth
who will be shot through
by its incredibility.

The wind is wild in empty space…
Try to live believing in stability:
that every moment is a loss.
Every moment is a mystery.

   1982

* * *

То облава, то потрава.
Выжил только третий справа.
Фотография стара.
А на ней юнцов орава.
Довоенная пора.
Что ни имя, что ни дата –
Тень войны и каземата,
Каземата и войны.
Время тяжко виновато,
Что карало без вины,
Приговаривая к нетям.
Хорошо быть справа третьим,
Пережившим этот бред.
Но и он так смят столетьем,
Что живого места нет.

1983

* * *

Итак, место действия – дом на земле,
Дорога земная и город во мгле.
Итак, время действия – ночи и дни,
Когда зажигают и гасят огни
И в зимнюю пору, и летней порой.
И, что ни участник, то главный герой,
Идущий сквозь сумрак и свет напролом
Под небом, под Богом, под птичьим крылом.

1983

* * *

First they rounded them up, then came the killing.
The third from the right alone survived.
It's an old photograph,
there's a horde of young men in it.
It's from pre-war days.
Every name, every date
is in the shadow of war and prison.
The time is seriously guilty
of executing the innocent,
sentencing to non-existence.
It's good to be third from the right
and have survived the madness.
But he too is so crushed by the century
that there's no life left in him.

1983

* * *

So, the action takes place in a house on earth,
a road on earth and a city in the haze.
So, the action takes place in nights and days,
when the lamps are lit and put out
both in winter time and summer time.
Everyone who takes part is the main hero
going headlong through dusk and light,
under heaven, under God, under the bird's wing.

1983

81

* * *

А чем здесь платят за постой,
За небосвода цвет густой,
За этот свет, за этот воздух,
И за ночное небо в звёздах?
Всё даром, – говорят в ответ, –
Здесь даром всё: и тьма, и свет.
А впрочем, – говорят устало, –
Что ни отдай, всё будет мало.

1983

* * *

Не больно тебе, неужели не больно
При мысли о том, что судьба своевольна?
Не мука, скажи, неужели не мука,
Что непредсказуема жизни излука,
Что память бездонна, мгновение кратко?
Не сладко, скажи, неужели не сладко
Стоять над текучей осенней рекою,
К прохладной коре прижимаясь щекою?

1983

* * *

What do you pay to stay here,
for the thick colour of the heavens,
for this light, for this air,
for this sky at night with its stars?
'It's all for free' they answer,
all free here, both dark and light.
'However' they say tiredly,
'whatever you give will always be too little.'

1983

* * *

Do you not feel pain, feel pain
before the thought that fate is wilful?
Tell me is it not a torture, a torture
that the curve of life cannot be foretold,
that memory is bottomless, the moment short?
Tell me, is it not sweet, not sweet
to stand above the river flowing in autumn
pressing one's cheek to the cool bark?

1983

* * *

Маме

Прости меня, что тает лед.
Прости меня, что солнце льёт
На землю вешний свет, что птица
Поет. Прости, что время длится,
Что смех звучит, что вьется след
На той земле, где больше нет
Тебя. Что в середине мая
Все зацветет. Прости, родная.

1984

* * *

По какому-то тайному плану
Снег засыпал и лес и поляну,
Берега водоёмов и рек.
Скоро кончится нынешний век,
Век двадцатый с рожденья Христова…
А пока половина шестого
Или где-то в районе шести.
И, часы позабыв завести,
Занят мир увлекательным делом:
Тихо пишет по белому белым.

1985

* * *

To my Mama

Forgive me that ice melts.
Forgive me that the sun pours
spring light on the earth, that a bird
sings. Forgive the lingering time,
the sound of laughter, the twisting of tracks
on that earth where you are no longer.
That everything will burst into blossom
in the middle of May. Forgive, my dear one.

1984

* * *

According to some secret plan
snow was strewn over the forest and glade,
the banks of watering-holes and rivers.
This century will soon be over,
the twentieth from the birth of Christ...
And now it's only five thirty,
or round about six.
Having forgotten to wind the clock,
the world is engaged in absorbing business:
quietly writing white on white.

1985

* * *

Слово – слеза, но без соли и влаги.
Слово – огонь, не спаливший бумаги.
Слово условно, как поза и жест:
Любят и гибнут, не сдвинувшись с мест.
Слово надежды и слово угрозы,
Точно скупые античные позы…
Дело зашло за порог болевой.
Вот и свидетельство боли живой:
Десять попарно рифмованных строчек
С нужным количеством пауз и точек.

1985

* * *

Высота берется с лёту.
Не поможет ни на йоту,
Если ночи напролёт
До измоту и до поту
Репетировать полёт.

Высота берется сходу.
Подниматься к небосводу
Шаг за шагом день и ночь –
Всё равно, что в ступе воду
Добросовестно толочь.

Высота берется сразу.
Не успев закончить фразу
И земных не кончив дел,
Ощутив полёта фазу,
Обнаружишь, что взлетел.

1986

* * *

A word is a tear but without salt and moisture.
A word is a fire that does not burn the paper.
The word is conditional, like a pose or a gesture:
they love and perish, yet are fixtures.
Word of hope and word of menaces,
like miserly antique poses...
The matter has gone beyond the threshold of pain.
This is the evidence of the living pain:
ten lines rhyming in couplets
with the necessary quantity of pauses and uplets.

1985

* * *

Height is gained immediately.
It doesn't help one iota
if the flight is rehearsed
right through the night
till exhaustion, till sweat breaks out.

Height is gained without a pause.
To rise to the heavens
pace after pace, night and day,
is the same as honestly
milling the wind.

Height is gained at once.
Not managing to finish the phrase,
not having finished your business on earth:
you feel suddenly the flight's phase,
you discover that you have taken wing.

1986

* * *

Поющий циферблат. Крылатые часы.
– Скажи, который час?
– Час утренней росы.
Час утренней росы и птичьих голосов.
Волшебные часы. Точнее нет часов.
– Живя по тем часам, скажи, который час?
– Тот самый заревой, когда Всевышний спас
Нас, грешных, от тоски, вручив бесценный клад:
Крылатые часы, поющий циферблат.

1987

* * *

Смертных можно ли стращать?
Их бы холить и прощать,
Потому, что время мчится
И придётся разлучиться.
И тоски не избежать.
Смертных можно ль обижать,
Изводить сердечной мукой
Перед вечною разлукой?

1987

* * *

A singing clockface. Winged hours.
'Tell me what time it is ?'
'The hour of morning dew,
the hour of morning dew and birds' voices.
Magical hours, rather no hours.'
'Since you live by that clock, tell me what time it is?'
'That same dawn hour, when the Almighty saved us
sinners from longing, entrusting to us a priceless treasure,
winged hours, a singing clockface.'

1987

* * *

Is it possible to scare mortals?
They should be cared for and forgiven
because time rushes by
and there'll be a time to part.
Anguish cannot be avoided.
Is it possible to hurt mortals,
to torment them with sufferings of the heart
before eternal parting?

1987

* * *

Мелким шрифтом в восемь строк
Про арест на долгий срок,
Про ежовщину и пытки,
Про побега две попытки,
Про поимку и битьё,
Про дальнейшее житьё
С позвоночником отбитым –
Сухо, коротко, петитом.

1987

* * *

И в черные годы блестели снега,
И в чёрные годы пестрели луга,
И птицы весенние пели,
И вешние страсти кипели.
Когда под конвоем невинных вели,
Деревья вишнёвые нежно цвели,
Качались озёрные воды
В те чёрные, чёрные годы.

1989

* * *

Eight lines in small script
about an arrest and a long term,
about Yezhovism and torture,
about two attempts to escape,
about capture and beatings,
about further living
with a smashed backbone,
dryly, briefly, by the prayer book.

    1987

* * *

The snow sparkled even in the black years,
the meadows were bright even in the black years,
the spring birds sang,
the vernal passions boiled.
When they led away the innocent under guard
the cherry trees were blossoming tenderly,
the waters of the lakes rippled
in those black, black years.

    1989

* * *

Из пышного куста акации, сирени,
Где круто сплетены и ветви, и листва,
Из пышного куста, его глубокой тени
Возникли мы с тобой, не ведая родства.
Дышало всё вокруг акацией, сиренью,
Акацией, грозой, акацией, дождём...
Ступив на первый круг, поддавшись нетерпенью,
Пустились в дальний путь. Скорей. Чего мы ждём?
И каждый божий день – посул и обещанье.
И каждый новый день и каждый новый шаг...
Откуда же теперь тоска и обнищанье,
Усталость и тоска, отчаянье и мрак?
А начиналось так: ветвей переплетенье,
И дышит всё вокруг сиренью и грозой,
И видя наш восторг, шумит листва в смятенье,
И плачет старый ствол смолистою слезой.
Неужто лишь затем порыв и ожиданье,
Чтоб душу извели потери без конца?
О, ливень проливной и под дождём свиданье,
О, счастье воду пить с любимого лица.

1989

* * *

From the splendid acacia and lilac bushes,
where branches and leaves are sharply intertwined,
from the splendid bush and its deep shade
we arose you and I, not knowing our origins.
All around breathed out acacia and lilac,
acacia, storm, acacia, rain.
Having set out on the first circle, impatiently
we went forth on the long journey.
Quick, what are we waiting for?
Every God's day held a promise, something special.
Every new day and every new step...
Why is there yearning and impoverishment now,
tiredness and yearning, despair and dark?
This is how it started: the intertwining of branches
and all around breathed out lilac and storm,
seeing our rapture the confusion of leaves rustled
and the old trunk cried with a resinous tear.
Was this uprush and waiting only in order that
losses without end should waste the soul?
Oh, the flooding downpour and a meeting in the rain,
oh, what happiness to drink water from a loved one's face.

1989

* * *

Шуршат осенние дожди,
Целуя в темя.
Ещё немного подожди,
Коль терпит время.
Ещё немного поброди
Под серой тучей,
А вдруг и правда впереди
Счастливый случай,
И всё текущее не в счёт –
Сплошные нети.
А вдруг и не жил ты ещё
На белом свете,
Ещё и музыка твоя не зазвучала…
Надежду робкую тая,
Дождись начала.

1989

* * *

The autumn rains rustle,
kissing the crown of the head.
Wait a little longer
if time will be patient.
Wander a little
under the black cloud,
and what if really
a happy incident is ahead,
and all that's happening doesn't count –
a mass of nos.
And what if you have never yet lived
in this wide world.
Your music has not yet rung out...
Wait for the beginning,
hiding your timid hopes.

1989

POEMS OF THE 90s

* * *

Плывут неведомо куда по небу облака.
Какое благо иногда начать издалека,
И знать, что времени у нас избыток, как небес,
Бездонен светлого запас, а чёрного в обрез.
Плывут по небу облака, по небу облака…
Об этом первая строка и пятая строка,
И надо медленно читать и утопать в строках,
И между строчками витать в тех самых облаках,
И жизнь не хочет вразумлять и звать на смертный бой,
А только тихо изумлять подробностью любой.

1990

* * *

Мемуары, флёр и дымка.
Тайна выцветшего снимка.
Дни текли, года летели,
Было все на самом деле
Прозаичнее и жестче,
И циничнее, и проще,
И сложней, и несуразней,
В сотни раз многообразней.
Ну а память любит дымку,
Снимок тот, где все в обнимку.
Там скруглила, там смягчила,
Кое-где слезой смочила,
Кое-где ошиблась в дате,
А в итоге, в результате
Обработки столь коварной
У былого – вид товарный.

1990

* * *

The clouds fly across the sky to God knows where.
What a blessing it is to sometimes start from a distance
and know that we have time in abundance, like the heavens
the supply of brightness is bottomless and there's no black to spare.
The clouds fly across the sky, clouds across the sky...
The first and fifth lines tell of this,
and one has to read slowly and draw in the lines
and to hover in these same clouds between the lines.
Life does not want to instruct and call to the deadly battle,
but only to quietly astound with any detail.

1990

* * *

Memoirs, veil and haze.
The secret of a faded photograph.
The days flowed, the years flew by,
everything was in fact
more prosaic and harsher,
more cynical and simpler,
more complex and more absurd,
a hundred times more varied,
well, memory loves a haze,
that photograph where everyone is embracing.
There it calmed, there it softened,
somewhere it's moistened by a tear,
somewhere there's a mistake in the date,
and to sum up, as a result
of such crafty treatment
the past is ready for sale.

1990

* * *

Мильон оранжевых штрихов,
Меж ними – просинь.
Не надо более стихов
Писать про осень.

Она до самых до небес
Давно воспета,
На тьму лирических словес
Наложим вето.

Не станем более плести
Словесной пряжи,
И вздор восторженный нести
В безумном раже…

Но все слова, какие есть,
Опять рифмую,
Им не умея предпочесть
Любовь немую.

1992

* * *

A million orange streaks,
between them a tinge of blue.
No need to write
any more poems about autumn.

It has long ago been sung
to the very skies.
Let's exercise our veto
on the myriad lyrical words.

We won't weave any more
the words' yarn,
and bear rapturous rubbish
in a crazed rage.

But I rhyme again
all the words that exist,
unable to prefer to them
a love that's wordless.

1992

* * *

На крыше – мох и шишки,
Под ней – кусок коврижки
И чайник на плите…
Предпочитаю книжки
Извечной суете.
Продавленный диванчик,
Да в поле одуванчик,
Который поседел.
Набрасываю планчик
Своих насущных дел:
Полить из лейки грядку,
И написать в тетрадку
Слова, строку вия,
И разгадать загадку
Земного бытия.

1992

* * *

Moss and fir cones on the roof,
under it – a piece of gingerbread
and a tea-kettle on the stove…
I prefer books
to age-old fussing.
A squashed little sofa
and in the field the dandelions
which have turned grey.
I am dashing off the plan
of my daily tasks:
to water the flower-bed from the can
and to write in the notebook
words, weaving the line
and to unravel the enigma
of existence on earth.

   1992

* * *

Памяти Юрия Карабчиевского

Опять утрата и урон,
Опять прощанье,
И снова время похорон
И обнищанья.

От боли острой и тупой
Беззвучно вою,
И говорю не то с собой,
Не то с тобою.

Я говорю тебе: "Постой.
Постой, не надо.
Быть может, выход есть простой,
Без дозы яда."

Ты мёртвый узел разрубил
Единым махом,
В земле, которую любил,
Оставшись прахом.

1992

* * *

In memory of Yuri Karabchievsky

Again loss and abandonment,
again farewell,
and once more the funeral time
and impoverishment.

I howl without a sound
from sharp and dull pain,
and I talk to myself
and I talk to you.

I say to you: 'Stop.
Stop. Don't do it.
Perhaps there's a simple way out,
without a dose of poison.'

You cut the mortal knot
with one swipe,
and remained dust
in the earth you loved.

1992

* * *

Уйти легко, а вот остаться
На этом свете, то есть сдаться
На милость предстоящих лет
Не просто. Проще сдать билет.
И ни хлопот тебе, ни давки –
Сплошные радости неявки:
Не значусь, не принадлежу,
С опаской в завтра не гляжу.

1993

* * *

> Легкий крест одиноких прогулок…
> О.Мандельштам

Пишу стихи, причем по-русски,
И не хочу другой нагрузки,
Другого дела не хочу.
Вернее, мне не по плечу
Занятие иного рода.
Меня волнует время года,
Мгновенье риска, час души…
На них точу карандаши.
Карандаши. Не нож, не зубы.
Поют серебряные трубы
В соседнем жиденьком лесу,
Где я привычный крест несу
Своих лирических прогулок.
И полон каждый закоулок
Души томлением, тоской
По женской рифме и мужской.

1993

* * *

It's easy to go away. But to stay
in this world, that is to give oneself up
to the mercy of the years ahead
is not simple. It's much simpler to give up one's ticket.
No worries, no pressure –
continuous pleasure of not appearing:
I am not registered, I don't belong,
I don't look at tomorrow with caution.

1993

* * *

> *The light cross of lonely strolls…*
> O. Mandelstam

I write poems, what's more in Russian,
and I don't want any other work load,
I don't want any other job.
Honestly I don't want to shoulder
any other enterprise.
The time of the year involves me,
the moment of risk, the hour of the soul…
I sharpen my pencils on them.
Pencils. Not knife or teeth.
The silver trumpets sing
in the frail neighbouring forest
where I will carry my usual cross
of lyric-making strolls.
Each backstreet is full
of the torment of the soul and yearning
for feminine and masculine rhymes.

1993

* * *

Опять минуты роковые.
Опять всей тяжестью на вые
Стоит История сама
И сводит смертного с ума,
И гнет деревья вековые.

И снова некогда дышать
И надо срочно поспешать
В необходимом направленьи,
Осуществляя становленье
И помогая разрушать.

А что до жизни до самой –
То до нее ли, милый мой?
И думать не моги об этом:
Мятеж весной, реформы – летом,
И перевыборы зимой.

1993

* * *

Again the fateful minutes.
Again History itself stands
with its full weight on the neck
and drives mortals mad
and bends the ancient trees.

Once more there's no time to breathe
and one has to immediately hurry
in a necessary direction,
realizing what's coming into being
and helping to destroy.

As to life itself,
you have no time to live,
you shouldn't even think of it
because there is a revolt in spring,
reforms in summer and re-elections in winter.

1993

* * *

В этой области скорби и плача,
Где эмблемою – череп и кол,
Мы привыкли, что наша задача
Наименьшее выбрать из зол.

Мы усвоили: только лишь крестный,
Крестный путь и достоин и свят,
В канцелярии нашей небесной
Канцелярские крысы сидят.

Ты спроси их: "Нельзя ли без муки?
Надоело, что вечно тоска".
Отмахнутся они от докуки,
Станут пальцем крутить у виска.

1993

* * *

Живем себе, не ведаем
В какую пропасть следуем
И в середине дня
Сидим себе, обедаем,
Тарелками звеня.

И правильно, без паники,
Ведь мы не на Титанике,
А значит, время есть
И чай допить и пряники
Медовые доесть.

1994

* * *

In this province of mourning and lamentation,
where the skull and the stake are emblems,
we got used to the fact that our task
was to pick the lesser evil.

We realized that only the Way of the Cross,
of the Cross is worthy and sacred,
in our heavenly chancery
sit only chancery rats.

You, ask them: 'Is it possible without suffering?
I'm fed up with this eternal anguish.'
They'll brush away the tiresome request
and start to screw their finger at the temple.

   1993

* * *

We live our life, not knowing
what abyss we are tracking
and in the middle of the day
we sit ourselves down and have lunch
and the plates rattle.

Correctly, without panic –
after all we're not on the Titanic,
so there's time
to drink down our tea
and eat the honey cake.

   1994

111

* * *

И ты попался на крючок,
И неба светлого клочок
Сиял, пока крючок впивался
И ты бессильно извивался,
Стремясь на волю, дурачок.
Тебе осталось лишь гадать
Зачем вся эта благодать,
И для чего тебя вдруг взяли,
Из тьмы беспамятства изъяли,
Решив земное имя дать.

1994

* * *

Кнутом и пряником. Кнутом
И сладким пряником потом.
Кнутом и сдобною ватрушкой…
А ежели кнутом и сушкой,
Кнутом и корочкой сухой?
Но вариант совсем плохой,
Когда судьба по твари кроткой –
Кнутом и плеткой, плеткой, плеткой.

1994

* * *

You got hooked
and a rag of bright sky
shone, while the little hook bit in
and you flailed around powerlessly,
striving for freedom, little fool.
You were left only to guess
why there is so much grace
and why you had suddenly been taken,
and they'd grabbed you out of the dark of the unconscious,
having decided to give you an earthly name.

1994

* * *

The whip and the honeycake. The whip
and then the sweet honeycake.
The whip and the rich cheese-cake...
If it's the whip and the roll
then why not the whip and the dry crust.
But this variant is very bad
when fate rules a gentle creature
with the whip and lash, lash, lash.

1994

* * *

В машинном рёве тонет зов,
И вместо дивной кантилены
Звучит надсадный вой сирены
И визг безумных тормозов.
И все же надо жить и петь,
Коль петь однажды подрядился,
И надо верить, что родился,
Чтобы от счастья умереть.

1994

* * *

Ждали света, ждали лета,
Ждали бурного расцвета
И благих метаморфоз,
Ждали ясного ответа
На мучительный вопрос.
Ждали сутки, ждали годы
То погоды, то свободы,
Ждали, веря в чудеса,
Что расступятся все воды
И дремучие леса…

А пока мы ждали рая,
Нас ждала земля сырая.

1995

114

* * *

The call drowns in the roar of the engine
and instead of the wonderful cantilena
the heavy howl of the siren is heard
and the squeal of crazed brakes.
But still you have to live and sing,
since once you have rallied yourself to sing,
you have to believe that you have been born
so as to die of happiness.

1994

* * *

They waited for light, waited for summer,
waited for the stormy blossoming
and graceful metamorphosis,
they waited for a clear answer
to the tormenting question.
They waited days, they waited years
for the right weather, for freedom,
they waited, believing in miracles,
that all waters would part
and the dense forest...

And while we were waiting for heaven
the damp earth awaited us.

1995

* * *

Заполним форму: год рожденья –
То бишь начало наважденья,
Начало бреда или сна…
Задача, кажется, ясна.
А в той графе, что ниже даты,
Дадим свои координаты;
Левее – пол; каких кровей
Укажем ниже и правей,
И роспись. Что, теперь яснее
И жизнь и как справляться с нею?

1995

* * *

Откуда ты?
Как все – из мамы,
Из темноты, из старой драмы,
Из счастья пополам с бедой,
Из анекдота с бородой.
Ну а куда?
Туда куда-то,
Где все свежо: цветы и дата,
И снег, и елка в Новый год,
И кровь, и боль, и анекдот.

1996

* * *

Let's fill in the form: date of birth –
that's the start of the delusion,
the start of delirium or dream…
The problem is clear, it seems.
And in the box below the date
we give our address and phone number;
on the left – our sex, lower on the right
we give our nationality,
then the signature. Well, is life clearer
now and how to cope with it?

1995

* * *

Where are you from?
Like everybody from Mama,
from darkness, from the old drama,
from happiness shared with disaster,
from a bearded anecdote.
Where to then?
To somewhere there,
where it's all fresh: flowers and a special date
and snow and a Christmas tree at New Year,
and blood, and pain and an anecdote.

1996

'Все страньше и страньше…'
Алиса в стране чудес

Все страньше жизнь моя и страньше,
Еще странней она, чем раньше,
Еще причудливей, чудней,
Еще острей тоска по ней -
– Чудной и чудной. Что же дальше?
А дальше – тишина, стена…
Смотри-ка, лампа зажжена
В чужом окне, где жизнь чужая
Проходит, старый провожая
И привечая новый миг.
Попробуй не сорвись на крик
И не воскликни: "Стой, мгновенье,
Постой", но ветра дуновенье
Возможно ли остановить?
Сухие губы шепчут: "Пить".
А может, "Жить". Дадут напиться,
Но жажда вряд ли утолится.
И длится бег ночей и дней,
Чей тайный смысл все темней,
А видимый и чужд и странен…
Любой из нас смертельно ранен
И мучим жаждой без конца,
А из тяжелого свинца
Небесного все льют живые
Живые воды дождевые.

1996

* * *

My life is curiouser and curiouser,
even stranger than before,
more odd, more wonderful,
my longing for it is even sharper,
miraculous, wonderful. What lies ahead?
Silence, the wall…
Look, the lamp is lit
by another's window, where a stranger's life
continues, accompanying the old
and greeting the new moment.
Try not to scream out
or exclaim: 'Stop, moment,
stop' but can one stop
the moaning of the wind?
Dry lips whisper: 'Give me a drink'
or perhaps: 'Give me a life'. They give us a drink
but my thirst is not really quenched.
The race of nights and days goes on,
whose secret sense is darker still
and the visible is alien and strange.
Any of us is mortally wounded
and tortured by endless thirst,
and the living, living rain water
pours down from the heavy leaden skies.

1996

* * *

И лишь в последний день творенья
Возникло в рифму говоренье,
Когда Господь на дело рук
Своих взглянул, и в нем запело
Вдруг что-то, будто бы задело
Струну в душе, запело вдруг,
Затрепетало и зажглось,
И все слова, что жили розно,
"О, Господи", – взмолились слёзно, –
"О, сделай так, чтоб все сошлось,
Слилось, сплелось." И с той поры
Трепещет рифма, точно пламя,
Рождённое двумя словами
В разгар Божественной игры.

1997

* * *

Дни тяжелы и неподъёмны.
Казалось бы, светлы, бездонны,
Легки – и всё же тяжелы.
Столь ощутимы и объёмны,
А догорят – и горсть золы.
И как нести всю тяжесть эту:
Весомых дней, текущих в Лету,
Событий иллюзорный вес,
Покров небес, которых нету, –
Аквамариновых небес.

1998

* * *

It was on the very last day of creation
that speech rose into rhyme,
when the Lord looked at
the work of His hands and suddenly something
sang in Him, as though a string was touched
in the soul and began to sing all at once:
it trembled and caught fire
and all the words, that had lived apart,
prayed through tears: 'O Lord,
O make it so that all can come together,
fuse, interweave.' From that time forwards
rhyme trembles like a flame,
born of two words,
at the height of the Divine game.

1997

* * *

Heavy days that can't be raised.
They seem to be bright, bottomless,
light, but nonetheless they are heavy.
So tangible and voluminous,
yet they burn down into a handful of ash.
How to carry all this heaviness:
weighty days, flowing to Lethe,
the illusory weight of events,
the covering of the heavens that don't exist,
the aquamarine heavens.

1998

* * *

Не стоит жить иль все же стоит –
Неважно. Время яму роет,
Наняв тупого алкаша.
Летай, бессмертная душа,
Пока пропойца матом кроет
Лопату, глину, тяжкий труд
И самый факт, что люди мрут…
Летай душа, какое дело
Тебе во что оденут тело
И сколько алкашу дадут.
Летай, незримая, летай,
В полёте вечность коротай,
В полёте, в невесомом танце,
Прозрачнейшая из субстанций,
Не тай, летучая, не тай.

1998

* * *

А что там над нами в дали голубой?
Там ангел с крылами, там ангел с трубой,
Там в ангельском облике облако, о!
Такое текучее, так далеко,
Как прошлое наше, как наше "потом",
Как дом самый давний, как будущий дом,
Верней, домовина. Откуда нам знать
Куда уплывает небесная рать,
Какими ветрами он будет разбит,
Тот ангел, который беззвучно трубит,
Тот ангел, который не ангел, а лишь
Сгущение воздуха, горняя тишь.

1999

* * *

It's not worth living or still it is –
it's not important. Time digs a pit,
having hired a thick clay.
Fly immortal soul,
before the drunkard covers with swear words
the spade, the clay, the heavy work
and the very fact that all people die…
Fly soul, what business is it
of yours what the body is clothed in
and how much money they give the clay?
Fly, invisible one, fly,
shorten eternity in your flight,
in your flight, your weightless dance,
most transparent of substances,
don't vanish, flying one, don't vanish.

    1998

* * *

What is there overhead in the pale blue distance?
There is a winged angel, there is an angel with a trumpet,
and in the angel's aspect there is a cloud!
So flowing, so distant,
like our past, like our 'later',
like the oldest home, like the future home,
or rather the coffin-home. How can one know
where the heavenly host is floating away,
by what winds it will be smashed?
That angel, who trumpets noiselessly,
that angel who is not an angel, but just
a thickening of the air, a sublime silence.

    1999

УРОК АНГЛИЙСКОГО

А будущее все невероятней,
Его уже почти что не осталось,
А прошлое – оно все необъятней,
Жила-была, вернее, жить пыталась,
Всё тащим за собой его и тащим,
Всё чаще повторяем "был", чем "буду"…
Не лучше ль толковать о настоящем:
Как убираю со стола посуду,
Хожу, гуляю, сплю, тружусь на ниве…
– На поле? – Нет, на ниве просвещенья:
Вот аглицкий глагол в инфинитиве –
– Скучает он и жаждет превращенья.
To stand – стоять. Глаголу не стоится,
Зеленая тоска стоять во фрунте,
Ему бы всё меняться да струиться
Он улетит, ей-Богу, только дуньте.
А вот и крылья – shall и will – глядите,
Вот подхватили и несут далёко…
Летите, окрылённые, летите,
Гляжу во след, с тоскою вперив око
В те дали, в то немыслимое фьюче,
Которого предельно не хватает…
Учу словцу, которое летуче,
И временам, что вечно улетают.

1999

ENGLISH LESSON

The future is more and more incredible,
there's almost nothing left of it,
and the past is more and more incomprehensible,
(once I lived, or rather tried to live),
we drag it after us constantly
and more often repeat 'I was' rather than 'I will'…
Isn't it better to speak about the present:
how I take the plates from the table,
I go, stroll, sleep, work in the field…
'In the cornfield?' No, in the field of education.
Here is the English verb in the infinitive –
it is bored and thirsts for transformation.
To stand: the verb can't stand,
there is a green longing to stand at the front,
it wants to change and stream.
It flies away – you just have to blow on it.
Here are the wings – 'shall' and 'will', look
they have caught on and carry far away.
Fly, winged ones, fly.
I look after them fastening my gaze
on these distances, on that inconceivable future,
which we desperately lack.
I teach the word that is flying,
and the tenses, that eternally confuse past and future.

1999

* * *

Oh, I believe in yesterday
The Beatles

Пели "Yesterday", пели на длинных волнах,
Пели "Yesterday", так упоительно пели,
И пылали лучи, что давно догорели,
Пели дивную песню о тех временах,
Полупризрачных тех, где всегда благодать,
Где пылают лучи, никогда не сгорая…
Да хранит наша память подобие рая,
Из которого нас невозможно изгнать.

1999

* * *

Я опять за своё, а за чьё же, за чьё же?
Ведь и Ты, Боже мой, повторяешься тоже,
И сюжеты Твои не новы,
И картинки Твои безнадёжно похожи:
Небо, морось, шуршанье травы…
Ты – своё, я – своё, да и как же иначе?
Дождь идёт – мы с Тобою сливаемся в плаче.
Мы совпали. И как не совпасть?
Я – подобье Твоё, и мои неудачи –
Лишь Твоих незаметная часть.

1999

* * *

Oh, I believe in yesterday.
                    The Beatles

They were singing 'Yesterday', singing it on the long waves,
singing 'Yesterday' intoxicatingly,
and those beams flared that had long ago burned down.
They were singing that wonderful song about those times,
half-ghostly, it was heavenly there,
where the rays flare and never burn out.
Let our memory preserve that likeness of paradise
from which we can't ever be thrown out.

   1999

* * *

I'm on about my own stuff again, and again,
but you see, You too, O God, repeat yourself,
and Your subjects are not new,
and Your pictures are hopelessly similar:
sky, drizzle, rustle of grass…
You have Your own, I my own, how could it be otherwise?
The rain falls – together we merge in the crying.
We have coincided – how could we not?
I am in Your likeness and my failures
are only an unnoticeable part of Yours.

   1999

* * *

С землёй играют небеса
И дразнят, и грозят обвалом,
Грозят в пожаре небывалом
Спалить жилища и леса.
А в тусклый день – они опять
Покровом серым и смиренным
Висят над этим миром бренным,
И слёз небесных не унять.

1999

* * *

На линии огня, огня,
Где плавится остаток дня
И полыхает, полыхает
И постепенно затухает,
Всевышний, не щади меня!
Пускай сгорит в Твоём огне
Всё опостылевшее мне
Во мне самой. Но если что-то
Ещё пригодное для взлёта
Откроешь Ты на глубине
На самой… Но чего хочу?
Советую Тебе, учу…

1999

* * *

The heavens are playing with the earth,
teasing, threatening a landslide,
they threaten to set fire
to the dwellings and forests – in a fantastic fire.
And on a dull day they hang again
over this mortal world
like a grey, humble shroud
and there's no soothing the tears of the heavens.

1999

* * *

Almighty, do not have mercy on me,
on the line of fire, of fire,
where the remains of the day melt
and blaze, blaze
and gradually die down.
Let all that has grown hateful to me
in my self burn in the fire.
But if You discover something
in the very depth that is still worthy
for flight… But what do I want?
I advise You, I teach…

1999

LARISSA MILLER is a major Russian lyrical poet and author of many short stories, essays and articles in periodicals, and of fourteen books, one in English translation (*Dim and Distant Days*, Glas, 2000). A member of the Union of Russian Writers since 1979, and of the Russian Pen-Centre since 1992, she was shortlisted in 1999 for the State Prize of the Russian Federation, having been nominated for the prize by the famous literary almanac *Novyi Mir*. Many poems by Larissa Miller have been set to music, in Russia by Michael Prikhod'ko (who has released three discs of songs to Miller's words), and in the UK by Helen Chadwick. In 2003, 49 of Larissa Miller's poems were put together as a theatrical 'Poetical Performance' which played at various Moscow theatres.

Born in 1940 Larissa Miller graduated from the Foreign Languages Institute in Moscow and for many years worked as a teacher of English, but since 1980 she has been teaching a women's musical gymnastics system named after its creator, the renowned Russian dancer Lyudmila Alexeeva.

RICHARD MCKANE was born in 1947 and read Russian at Oxford, his *Selected Poems of Anna Akhmatova* (Penguin / OUP) appearing in 1969. He lived in Turkey for six years in the 1970s, working on an archaeological dig in Kandahar, Afghanistan for some of this time. In 1978 he was awarded the Hodder Fellowship at Princeton University where he met his former wife Elizabeth, with whom he later he brought out Mandelstam's *Moscow and Voronezh Notebooks*.

For over eighteen years, he worked as an interpreter from, and into, Turkish and Russian at the Medical Foundation for the Care of Victims of Torture.

As a translator, Richard McKane, working with Ruth Christie, has brought out two selections of Oktay Rifat's work, *Voices of Memory* and *Poems* and, with Tâlat Halman, *Beyond the Walls: Poems of Nâzým Hikmet*; he has also translated the work of Nikolai Gumilyov, Olga Sedakova and Aronzon. As a poet, he has had two bilingual books published in Turkey, *Turkey Poems*

131

and *Coffee House Poems*, and a selection, *Amphora for Metaphors*, in New York.

Richard McKane has retired from interpreting, and now lives in the provinces, concentrating on his translation and poetry.

SASHA DUGDALE has published two poetry collections, *Notebook* (Carcanet / Oxford Poets, 2003) and *The Estate* (Carcanet / Oxford Poets, 2007). She translates Russian plays for several theatres in the UK and the USA, her translations including *Plasticine* by Vassilii Sigarev (winner of the Evening Standard New Play of the Year Award), *Terrorism* and *Playing the Victim* by the Presnyakov Brothers and Chekhov's *Cherry Orchard* (produced by BBC Radio in Autumn 2008).

Her translations of Russian poetry are published by Bloodaxe. The most recent, a collection of poetry by Elena Shvarts entitled *Birdsong on the Seabed* (2008), was a PBS Recommended Translation.